To our forebears the transformation in the landscape brought about by the building of the early railways must have been very difficult to comprehend. The construction of the various new road schemes of today is, perhaps, a parallel, although with hardly the same moral impact as the first railways. Unfortunately the development of the camera was towards the latter part of the nineteenth century and with most railways already built by this time views of railway construction are rare. Fortunately this was not the case with the section of line from Hurst Green Junction to Groombridge, the photograph showing one of the small steam engines belonging to the contractor, J.T. Firbank, at work in January 1887 on what is obviously temporary trackwork.

Junction of the new line with the existing railway at Hurst Green just south of Oxted. On the right is the existing main line from London towards Lingfield and East Grinstead whilst to the left is the new route to Groombridge.

The normally forgotten side of railway engineering, an occupation bridge, usually provided where a previous agricultural lane crossed the path of the railway. This is Grant's Lane bridge, again on the new line, the narrowness of the bridge accentuated by the height of the arch.

Just north of Edenbridge the S.E.C.R. Redhill to Tonbridge route passed over the Groombridge line, the new line immediately plunging into a tunnel at the same point. Showing up well is the ballast covering for the sleepers whilst the fish-plate joints are left clear, the South Eastern being one of many railway companies which followed this practice at the time.

The appropriately named Edenbridge Road which passes under the railway between Edenbridge Tunnel and Edenbridge Station. Edenbridge itself possessed two stations, one on the new line from Oxted to Groombridge and the other on the original South Eastern route between Redhill and Ashford. This is looking in the direction of the S.E.R. station.

Edenbridge, L.B. & S.C.R. station seen towards Oxted and with the whole area in markedly neat and tidy style. The substantial goods shed on the left reflects the importance of the railways for the transport of freight. The view was probably taken between January and October 1888.

After numerous delays the line as far south as Edenbridge was finally opened by the London, Brighton & South Coast Railway on 2nd January 1888 and eventually to Ashurst Junction on 1st October the same year. This view shows Edenbridge probably during the brief period it remained a terminus and with a number of goods wagons just discernible in the yard.

To avoid confusion with the neighbouring Edenbridge station on the South Eastern & Chatham Company's line, the Edenbridge on the Oxted line had the suffix 'Town' added from May 1896. This heavily retouched card shows a train from the direction of Hurst Green Junction entering the station.

(Lens of Sutton)

Railway Station, Edenbridge.
L. B. & S. C. Ry.

Next station south was Hever (for Hever Castle) and viewed south towards Cowden, probably just prior to opening. Wherever possible similar designs were used for the various buildings at all the stations. There is a marked similarity between the main station here and that at the next stopping place, Cowden.

3

Seen from the opposite side it is possible to pick out five members of the station staff, two on each platform and one just visible on the signal box steps. The station master resided on the upper floor of the station buildings whilst it was common practice to provide cottages for other railway staff close by the station.

Between Hever and Cowden was Markbeech Tunnel, 682 yards long and taking the railway under Markbeech Wood. The fresh construction is very apparent here with little vegetation at present growing against the cutting sides.

Cowden station opened to passengers on 1st October 1888, the neat and tidy appearance indicating this was perhaps imminent. Markbeech Tunnel, depicted in the previous view, is just out of sight around the curve towards Hever. Interestingly the platform surface would appear to be topped with gravel, although it is known that later a tarmac covering was provided.

Cowden again but this time south towards Ashurst. On the left the loading gauge was used to ensure that wagons were within limits and so could travel safely through the various bridges on the line. Different companies had slightly differing limits, the L.B. & S.C.R. being one of the narrowest routes.

A few years later what may well be an Oxted to Tunbridge Wells West train is entering Cowden station. (Lens of Sutton)

Cowden Station. L. B. & S. C. Ry.

As with the station buildings the goods yards at the various stations were similar although not all were originally provided with a goods shed. This is Ashurst. In the background is a team of horses hitched to a dray backed up against one of the wagons. As this was a rural area a local carrier was probably employed to collect and deliver goods in the immediate station area.

At the north end of the station the railway crossed the Mill Race from which the viaduct was named. Nearby the Mill Race connected with the River Medway which flowed parallel with the railway for some distance. The long time exposure necessary for the print has resulted in the water taking on a glazed appearance.

Ashurst Junction and the end of the new line. To the left is the route from Groombridge whilst that on the right goes to Eridge and eventually Polegate and Lewes. The wooden signal box controlling the junction is one of the many 'boxes on stilts' favoured by the L.B. & S.C.R. for many years.

Another new line of the 1880s was the joint Croydon, Oxted and East Grinstead Railway, which opened on 10th March 1884. The route was built jointly by the L.B. & S.C.R. and S.E.R. companies. Part of the route south of East Grinstead is now famous as the Bluebell Railway. This is St Margaret's Junction, East Grinstead just before the opening. The line on the left goes to the low level station with that on the right to the high level station. A platelayer's trolley can also just be seen through the arch leading to the high level station.

Finally on this sequence of railway construction I could not resist including a view of the magnificent brick retaining wall again on the Croydon, Oxted & East Grinstead Railway not far from St Margaret's Junction. The masonry was required to support the cutting walls whilst its series of neat arches perhaps typifies the care the Victorian engineers took in the design of even such ancillary structures.

'Gladstone' class 0-4-2 No.199 'Samuel Laing' depicted at an unknown location, probably around 1912. The 36 engines of this class were built between 1882 and 1891 for express passenger work, although with the rapid development of both traffic and engine design they were already relegated to secondary duties by the turn of the century. What is so surprising, however, is the pristine external condition. No.199 is in umber livery and fully lined out.

(Adrian Vaughan Collection)

By comparison this is the doyen of the class No.172 'Littlehampton' at what may well be East Grinstead in 1920. Against the view above the ravages of war have taken their toll with an all pervading covering of grime. With labour no longer either cheap or plentiful appearances would never return to what was regarded as the golden age of railways during the Edwardian era.

(Adrian Vaughan Collection)

The first public railway in Sussex had been the short Brighton to Shoreham route opened in May 1840. This was followed in September 1841 with the opening of the main line throughout from London to Brighton where at the coastal resort a station was built in Queens Road truly in keeping with the grandeur of the town. For many years the tram terminus was adjacent to the railway station and so provided an early example of rail and road co-operation. Today the buildings on the left have been demolished and replaced by a 'bus terminus.

(Reg Randell Collection)

Inside the terminus and with the Victorian love of ornate ironwork well depicted in the scrollwork above the platform entrance. The reference to 'Main' refers to the line to London whilst 'East Coast' relates to trains destined towards Lewes and Hastings. Visible on the platform is a private horse drawn carriage: the railway offered a service for transporting such vehicles on board a special truck attached to the rear of the train.

(Lens of Sutton)

Against a forest of mechanical signals, 'C1' 0-6-0 No.427 stands at Brighton around the turn of the century. This engine was built in May 1884 at a cost of £2,245, excluding the tender, and survived in service until March 1911. (L.G.R.P.)

Outside the Brighton station and with the overall roof in the background. The L.B. & S.C.R. adopted the practice of naming most of their passenger engines albeit with the name just painted on. B4, 4-4-0 No.42 'His Majesty' and D3, 0-4-4T No.363 'Havant' are waiting to come off the shed just outside the station whilst alongside a group of men attend to the track.   (Lens of Sutton)

Another spotless engine, No.160, inside Brighton shed in June 1922.   (L.G.R.P.)

Controlling the movement of traffic in and out of the terminus at Brighton was a massive mechanical signal box, shown here with the running shed on the left and part of the locomotive works to the right. The engines are in the process of being moved from one side of the running lines to the other and so perhaps indicating No.271 is being returned to traffic after overhaul.

(M. Sumner Collection)

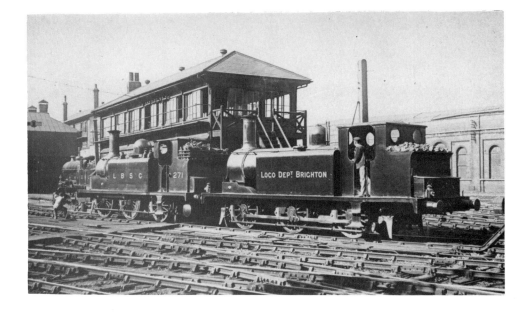

The north bound 'Sunny South Coast Express' leaving Brighton. This was a through service from the South Coast to the North Midlands and ran via Willesden and Clapham Junction to Brighton where the service divided with one portion going on to Eastbourne. The coaching stock is of London & North Western Railway origin.

(Lens of Sutton)

Dating from 1868, No.395 was the Bricklayers Arms (Willow Walk) shunter from 1868-1880. This unusual engine was built by the firm of Craven and originally carried the number 52. After working in the London area it was used on shunting duties at Newhaven for a time before going to Brighton, where the photograph was taken. It was finally laid aside in October 1893.　　　　(L.G.R.P.)

No.189 'Edward Blount' at speed on one of the prestige Pullman services near Preston Park just north of Brighton in 1900.

(L.G.R.P.)

In keeping with their surroundings the stations on the original main line were designed in ornate style, many with mock Tudor beams. Hassocks Gate was originally the first stopping place north of Brighton, but the suffix was dropped during late 1881. To reach this point the railway has had to pass through the South Downs via a succession of heavy earthworks. On the right the sign reads 'Hassocks Sale Yard' and indicates the station site was also used for a variety of auctions. This would make practical sense as an amount of sale goods would no doubt be transported to the site by rail and by holding the auction alongside the railway movement costs were kept to a minimum.

(Lens of Sutton)

As with the previous view of the 'down' side at Hassocks the 'up' side was again in mock Tudor style and included the station master's house on the left. On the station approach are a number of horse drawn vehicles one of which is an early public omnibus.

(Lens of Sutton)

Passenger facilities at Hassocks included up and down platforms with the surface it will be noticed unusually wide. In the background the South Downs may just be seen whilst nearer at hand the goods yard is at the end of the 'up' or London bound platform.

(Lens of Sutton)

'Atlantic' No.426 near Hassocks at the head of a 'down' Brighton express. (L.G.R.P.)

Just south of Wivelsfield Station was Keymer Junction and the point of divergence for the line to Lewes. Between 1862 and 1883 a station known as Keymer Junction existed on the curve of the Lewes line whilst a few years later from 1886 a new Keymer Junction station was brought into use on the main line to serve both routes. To add more confusion the name of this later station was changed to Wivelsfield from 1st July 1896.

A few years later and a new signalbox has replaced the former lofty structure. Passing by the Lewes line is a stopping service from Brighton to London. (Reg Randell Collection)

Another of the 'Atlantics', this time No.424, at the time un-named but later officially called 'Beachy Head', running non stop through Wivelsfield with the down 'Southern-Belle' express. This pullman train which ran between Victoria and Brighton was the fore-runner of the renowned 'Brighton Belle' electric service.   (Reg Randell Collection)

Staff of the engineers department dealing with an earth slip on the embankment at Wivelsfield station in February 1913.
(Reg Randell Collection)

Haywards Heath at 38 miles from London was the terminus of the main line for two months from July 1841. During this time and whilst work continued on the remaining distance to Brighton a horse drawn coach was available to convey passengers over the final stretch, but with the poor state of the roads the 18 miles took no less than two hours. The town of Haywards Heath owes much of its development to the railway, for at the time of opening it was basically open land with Cuckfield the nearest sizeable habitation three miles west. The view is taken from the top of the surrounding hills and shows the station with a yard full of wagons, probably around harvest time judging by the amount of hay and straw to be seen.   (Reg Randell Collection)

Between Haywards Heath and Balcombe the railway crosses the valley of the River Ouse by means of a masonry viaduct over ¼ mile long and the longest structure of this type on the original Brighton route.

(Reg Randell Collection)

The importance of Three Bridges as a junction began in 1848, seven years after the arrival of the main line, with the opening of the route to Horsham. Later still came the line to East Grinstead which also diverged from the Brighton route just south of the station. As was practice at the time some very tall signals were provided to control the junctions, the centre post for trains on the main line. The view shows the station before it was widened and includes a glimpse of the loco shed on the extreme left.   (Lens of Sutton)

A similar view but from a low angle and with one of the through trains from the L.&N.W.R. passing through en-route for Brighton. The engine is No.213 'Bessemer' of the B2 class introduced between 1895 and 1898 and intended for express passenger work.   (Lens of Sutton)

Inside the station at Three Bridges and looking north towards Gatwick and London. As with Hassocks this station had unusually wide platforms and the opportunity was taken to place two sets of seats parallel with the rails. In the background is the refreshment room and newspaper stall whilst under a magnifying glass a match salesman is also visible.   (Lens of Sutton)

Following rebuilding there were four through platform faces at Three Bridges together with a loop for the Horsham line. At the head of what is probably a stopping service to Brighton is 'D' class 0-4-2T No.258, originally named 'Cosham'.   (Lens of Sutton)

Holding up pedestrians in the centre of Crawley an unidentified E5 0-6-2T heads west away from the station and over the town level crossing towards Horsham. The lack of vehicular transport is perhaps the most obvious feature of the view although a bicycle can be seen leaning against the advertisement hoarding. The large building on the right is the Station Hotel.   (Lens of Sutton)

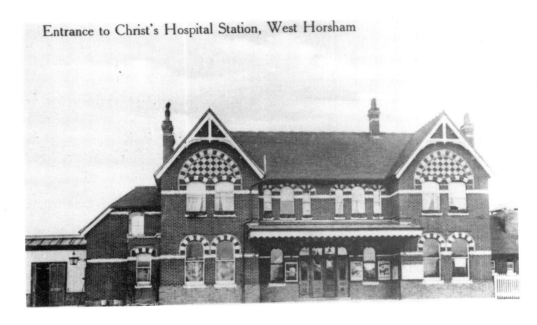

Entrance to Christ's Hospital Station, West Horsham

The famous school at Christ's Hospital was on the west of Horsham and considered too far out to be adequately served by the existing Horsham station. Accordingly a new station was provided and appropriately given the name of the school. The ornate main building was a replica of the actual college.

(Lens of Sutton)

Christ's Hospital was also the junction for the lines north to Guildford, west to Pulborough and south to Shoreham, trains for the latter using the double sided platform on the right. The habit of having two platform faces to one track was used at several stopping places on the L.B. & S.C.R., with the Bluebell Railway station at Horsted Keynes a well known example. (Lens of Sutton)

Christ's Hospital Station, West Horsham

WEST GRINSTEAD. LBSCR

Taking the line south from Christ's Hospital the second station reached was West Grinstead. Originally single track the route was doubled between 1877 and 1879. It was a useful diversionary route to the coast but a multitude of sharp curves and steep gradients precluded any attempt at high speed running. Entering an almost deserted station with what may well be a through train to the coast an 'E4' tank dwarfs its train. The numerous enamel adverts were a regular feature of the contemporary railway scene.

(Lens of Sutton)

The 'up' side approach at West Grinstead, complete with horse drawn cab. Of the 13 persons visible probably about half are railway employees, for as with the locomotive department in the days when labour was cheap each station boasted its own station master, porters, clerk and signalmen.

(Lens of Sutton)

Partridge Green station was in the centre of a farming community and saw considerable milk traffic for many years. The use of churns nowadays is but a memory. There was originally a low area of platform intended to facilitate the loading of wagons but this had been filled in by the turn of the century. Besides connecting the platforms the footbridge joined the side of the Steyning Road which ran parallel with the line for a short distance. The view is looking north towards London.

(Lens of Sutton)

Henfield station on the same line and viewed towards Christ's Hospital. Unusually for the period the scene is devoid of passengers. Partly hidden from view within the goods shed is No.223 'Balcombe' one of Stroudley's celebrated 'D' class of 0-4-2T engines of which 123 were built at Brighton Works between 1873 and 1887. From the photograph it is likely the engine is in the process of shunting the yard whilst its train waits in the platform. Journey times for passengers on several rural lines involved an average speed little quicker than the days of the stage-coach.

(Mowat Collection)

With a porter busy at his barrow 'D3' 0-4-4T 'Billingshurst' enters the station with a Shoreham train. The curved valance to the canopy is a particularly pleasing feature. In the background the signal has been raised above the height of the bridges to give as clear an indication as possible against a sky background.
(Lens of Sutton)

Probably to cope with increased traffic a new signal box was provided at Henfield in 1907. The signalman is proudly posing at the window.　　　　　(Lens of Sutton)

Largest of the stations on the Mid Sussex route from Christ's Hospital was Steyning. The town had its origins as a market town, and indeed for many years there was a regular cattle market alongside the railway. Here also good supplies of water were found beneath the railway and pumped into a storage tank alongside. The lattice type of footbridge was common on the railways in East Sussex although not all had the covering shown here.　　　　　(Lens of Sutton)

Last stopping place before the coast main line was Bramber where the main buildings were unusually placed at the north end of the 'up' platform. The view is towards Steyning. The print is taken from a copy of an old postcard on which the 'x' mark possibly indicated a relative of the original recipient.   (Lens of Sutton)

Back on the main line at Southwick on the coast route from Brighton to Chichester. This is the westbound approach side and with the cannon thought to commemorate the involvement of local troops in one of the African campaigns.   (Lens of Sutton)

SOUTHWICK. LBSCR.

East towards Brighton is Hove, at the time the view was taken a separate location in its own right but nowadays almost merged with its neighbour. The horse drawn vehicles are probably all taxis and indicating the period as around 1900. The view is of the 'down' or west bound side of the station.

(Lens of Sutton)

For many years the railways enjoyed an almost total monopoly of both passenger and goods transport, the delivery of goods to both commercial and private premises being a common if poorly recorded side of the business. Here though the camera has caught what was probably just one of many delivery drays operating from Hove. The vehicle was in the charge of two men who would operate within a given distance of the station. On the rear of the wagon a poster is advertising a special fast train from Brighton to Epsom for Derby Day at what appears to be 3/- return fare. (Lens of Sutton)

Some of the largest express tender engines owned by the L.B. & S.C.R. were the five 'H1' 'Atlantics' built in 1905/6. As constructed all were at first un-named although No.39 was designated 'La France' in 1909. This is the engine prior to 1909 and as would be expected polished to a high level of perfection. (Adrian Vaughan Collection)

Built by the independent Brighton & Dyke Railway Co., the 3½ mile branch of the same name was opened on 1-9-1887 running from Dyke Junction Halt (now known as Aldrington) on the main route between Hove and Brighton. The L.B. & S.C.R. operated the service from the outset and later used a steam railcar for a time although for most of its life the service was operated with conventional locomotive and carriages. (Lens of Sutton)

The promoters had hoped to attract day trippers to the high ground of the South Downs north of Brighton and although this was moderately successful the resultant traffic was very seasonal. Indeed with the exception of one intermediate halt which served a golf course all trade was handled at the terminus. The remoteness of the location is well displayed here with little to detract from the barren landscape. The view was probably taken not long after opening as the chalk embankment still appears fresh. Trains always ran from the Dyke to Brighton, the steep gradients associated with the branch well displayed to the right. (Lens of Sutton)

Unfortunately the advent of the motor coach and private car spelt an end to the little railway, which despite its remote location also handled freight. The South Downs were an inhospitable place during times of poor weather, a mist providing a sombre backcloth to this last view of the station.

(Lens of Sutton)

Another dead end line from Brighton was the 1½ mile Kemp Town branch, intended to provide a suburban service for the east side of the town. As with similar local schemes elsewhere it was an early casualty to competition from trams and buses. In happier times 'D' class 0-4-2T No.28 'Isfield' stands on its train waiting to return to the Central station. The chimney in the background was part of the 'Alpine Mills'. (L.G.R.P.)

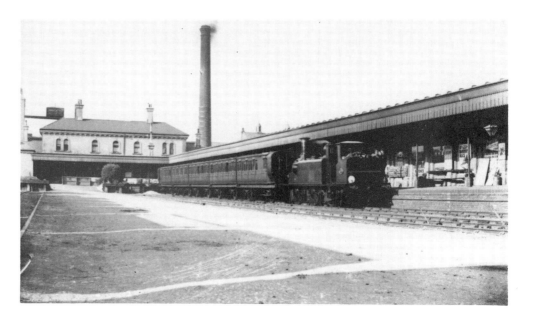

Railway Station, Lewes

The town of Lewes has had no less than three separate railway stations, the politics of railway construction in the 1800s meaning that the advent of a new line required a change in the available facilities. This is the third station of 1889 and situated in the 'V' of the junction between the lines from Brighton and Plumpton. With the exception of perhaps Eastbourne the ornate roof and pagoda was unique amongst the stations of East Sussex. (Lens of Sutton)

Seen this time from the actual junction, the train approaching is from the direction of Brighton and composed of very early stock. It is especially interesting to compare this view with that from a similar angle in the next photograph as development began to take place on the site. (Lens of Sutton)

The second station and already with a variety of additional buildings and facilities. Three engines can also be seen whilst in the centre a number of railway staff are engaged in moving quantities of luggage. (Pamlin Prints)

The rebuilt station again but this time from the Brighton end. Another of the double sided platforms was provided here. They were ideal for dealing with large numbers of passengers very quickly.   (Lens of Sutton)

'D' class 0-4-2T No.281 'Withyham' leaves Lewes heading east with a passenger train destined for Eastbourne and Hastings.
(Lens of Sutton)

A further stage in building and a view this time of the third station. The train just pulling away is a Victoria to Newhaven boat train special, with connections available from Dieppe to Paris.   (Lens of Sutton)

23

Prior to electrification many of the branch and stopping services in the county were in the hands of 'Terrier' tanks. An unidentified member of the class leaves the station with a stopping train for Cooksbridge and Plumpton.
(Reg Randell Collection)

A final view of Lewes with the line to Crowborough on the left and that to Hastings on the right. Alongside the track is a multiplicity of point rodding necessary with mechanical signalling whilst the signal gantry in the distance has a decidedly drunken appearance.
(Lens of Sutton)

An express of a century past with a 'down' Eastbourne train on the main coast line near Lewes, probably during the 1880s.
(Brighton Library)

The nearest the L.B. & S.C.R. reached to France, the terminal at Newhaven. On the left the railway continues along the coast to Seaford whilst straight ahead is the harbour referred to as the 'Continental Quay'. Just visible on the right is the front of the London-Paris hotel evidently in the process of being extended. (Lens of Sutton)

A London bound service waiting to leave Newhaven Harbour with an immaculate 'I3' 4-4-2T at the head. Here was another of the double sided platforms with the overall canopy providing a degree of protection from the weather. (Reg Randell Collection)

Complete with Pullman coach, an empty boat train special stands in one of the sidings alongside the terminal at Newhaven harbour, no doubt awaiting a return working to London. The first two vehicles are luggage vans and are necessary because of the amount of baggage the Victorian traveller would carry. (Lens of Sutton)

Terminus of the line at Seaford with a Lewes train waiting to depart. During the day the white discs and crosses indicated both the type of train and its destination whilst lamps were used at night. (Lens of Sutton)

S 5317 L.B.& S.C. RAILWAY STATION, SEAFORD.

Junction for the Eastbourne route was at Polegate and another location where one station had been replaced by another following the opening of a new connecting line. Depicted here is the second station which opened in 1881 just after the route north through Hailsham had been brought into use. On the far right a 'C3' class 0-6-0 is shunting the yard whilst both main lines are also occupied by trains. To complete the busy scene a tank engine waits in the 'up' loop on an Eastbourne to Tunbridge Wells service.

(Reg Randell Collection)

Polegate boasted a particularly ornate station, indeed today it is a listed structure and substantially unaltered. Following rationalisation of resources under BR the station has now been resited at its original location some yards distant. (Lens of Sutton)

The station at Hampden Park opened in January 1888 with the name Willingdon and was renamed in 1903. This is looking north towards Polegate showing how the footbridge was staggered so as to afford access to the respective platform buildings. On the left the main building is identical to that some miles away at Fittleworth on the line from Pulborough to Midhurst although on the opposite side the small shelter with its curved roof and overhanging valance is more unusual. As with many period views the costumes are worthy of a second glance.

(Lens of Sutton)

Arguably the most ornate of all L.B. & S.C.R. stations was the terminus at Eastbourne which dates from 1900, although the line to the town had opened many years earlier. The building was designed in keeping with the style of its surroundings whilst again the complete lack of almost all vehicle transport is in stark contrast with later years. Notice in particular the bath-chair parked by the near-side kerb. In the background is an open top bus which may well have been horse-drawn, the town of Eastbourne being the operator of the first municipal bus service in the country. (Lens of Sutton)

From the front and with the station design displaying its origins in contemporary Chinese style. An interesting feature is the number of cab porters waiting for any possible trade and with what may well be the cab inspector standing in the centre. (Lens of Sutton)

Inside the station at Eastbourne and with a rich variety of enamel notices on display. The Smith's bookstall remained on the same site for many years but was later moved to a different location although it has since reverted to nearly the same site.

(Lens of Sutton)

57 EASTBOURNE. — Interior of the Railway Station. — LL.

Posed on the turntable at the second Eastbourne shed around 1890 is No.209 'Devonshire'. The engine was then just eleven years old and had been built at Brighton. It survived until April 1901 having accrued a total mileage of some 767,662 miles.

(L.G.R.P.)

Viewed towards London and with a train approaching the terminus. The signal box controlled all movements in and out of the station — indeed it is still doing so in 1987. On the extreme left is the steam round-house with an engine alongside the coaling stage. (Lens of Sutton)

The 'Sunny South Coast' express leaving the terminus on 1st March 1905 with 'B2' 4-4-0, No.323 'William Cubitt' at the head. The train is made up of a number of L.N.W.R. vehicles and is bound for the Midlands.
(Ray Randell Collection)

Away from the public eye the railwaymen still maintained a pride in the job, the interior of this signal box for example shows the efforts of many hours with polish and burnisher. On the shelf the various instruments control movement between neighbouring signal boxes whilst the small brass circular repeaters show the position of signals otherwise invisible from the 'box. The lever tops are burnished until they shine and only ever moved with a duster to avoid leaving fingerprints.   (Adrian Vaughan Collection)

Steam on the main line to Brighton, with another 'Gladstone' 0-4-2 at the head of a London to Brighton train in 1920. The engine was formerly named 'Northcote' although by this time the painted splasher has been covered over. In charge on the footplate is Driver John Reade, the tender slightly unusual in that the wheels are fully exposed and have inside bearings. (Adrian Vaughan Collection)

Eastwards still on the coastal main line is Pevensey & Westham station, originally opened with the names in reverse order. The scene is towards Hastings. Unusually for the time the small yard appears somewhat untidy. Again there are a number of churns on the platform whilst beyond the footbridge is a level crossing open for road traffic.

(Lens of Sutton)

With the proximity of the railway to the shore between Pevensey and Hastings it was natural the railway company should try to exploit the advantages of the Sussex coast. Accordingly at Cooden signs were placed which pointed the traveller to the beach just a few hundred yards away, although it is appreciated none can be seen here! In the background it is possible to discern an open top tram on the rival service which operated from Cooden to Hastings. Originally opened as a Halt, the station was rebuilt and renamed Cooden Beach in 1935. (Lens of Sutton)

VIEW FROM STATION, COODEN.

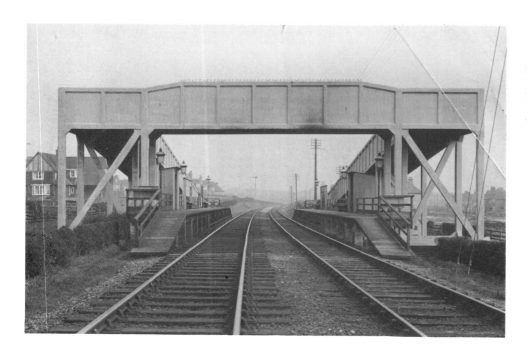

In an attempt to find an alternative to both timber and steel the L.B. & S.C.R. investigated the use of concrete as a building material. One of the first uses on the Brighton system was this footbridge at Collington between Cooden and Bexhill, photographed on 8-4-1921. (British Railways)

30

The L.B. & S.C.R. were amongst the pioneers in the use of steam railmotors — themselves the forerunners of today's multiple unit diesel and electric sets. This was one of the first railmotors operated by the Brighton company and which had the locomotive and coach permanently coupled. The unit is shown at Bexhill and operated the local service to Hastings and Eastbourne. (L.G.R.P.)

The L.B. & S.C.R. opened several small halts in an attempt to attract extra traffic. Many had short lives such as Glynne Gap Halt between Bexhill and (St Leonards) West Marina. The large building on the right is the Glynne Gap Gas Works with the sea out of sight on the left. This halt existed only from 1905 to 1915.   (Lens of Sutton)

Another railcar, this time at St Leonards station. Despite a promising start the units failed to live up to expectations. One of the main disadvantages was the fact that servicing had to be carried out at the engine shed where the coach portion became a magnet for dirt and grime. Only four vehicles were built and the last was withdrawn in 1931.
            (Reg Randell Collection)

Posed outside the engine shed at (St Leonards) West Marina is No.212 'Hartington'. The building on the left is the rear of the signal box whilst that to the right may well be the top of an earlier signal box now grounded and used as an office. (L.G.R.P.)

At the delightfully named Bopeep Junction the L.B. & S.C.R. came into direct contact with the S.E.R. route from Tunbridge Wells. This early view shows the layout in 1892 with the rival stations, West St Leonards and St Leonards West Marina respectively to right and left — the latter is just visible beyond the overbridge with the engine shed to the right of the line. The chalk cliffs so typical of the terrain are also discernible whilst on the S.E.R. line an early signal with arms for each direction but on the same post can be seen. (Lens of Sutton)

(18B)   BoPeep Junction.
         SER/LBSCR. 1892.

(6B)   Hastings Station. SER.
        1893.

Another early view, this time of Hastings station in 1893. The changes that have occurred on the railways since that time are obvious with the rolling stock in particular decidedly primitive. On the extreme right is a platform used by Brighton line trains whilst the remaining platform takes the line further east and eventually to Ashford. The engine shed is on the left hand side whilst the whole station was substantially altered when rebuilt in pseudo-concrete during the 1930s.

(Reg Randell Collection)

Hastings station with the nameboard clearly showing its origins to the South Eastern & Chatham Railway. (Reg Randell Collection)

(44B) Rye Station. SER. 1877.

The line from Hastings through Rye to Ashford was opened in 1851 and the short branch to Rye Harbour three years later in 1854. Shown is the typical South Eastern Railway feature of a staggered platform layout with a lack of any obvious signals.

(Lens of Sutton)

On the S.E.R. route north from Hastings is Crowhurst station, seen here from the passenger approach. The architecture is a marked contrast to the Brighton design.

(Lens of Sutton)

STATION ENTRANCE   CROWHURST

(16B) Battle Station. SER.
1872.

With its historical connections the station at Battle was built in charming contemporary style. This 1872 view was taken just 21 years after opening and shows a ballast covering above the sleepers. The practice continued for some years until it was realised that sleepers could rot away without being detected. (Lens of Sutton)

Robertsbridge was also the junction for the renowned Kent & East Sussex Light Railway part of which survives in preservation. Here though is a view of the main line station which again had a staggered platform layout. (Lens of Sutton)

(34B) Robertsbridge Station.
SER. 26th July 1888.

(19B) Etchingham Station.
SER.

Another of the original stations on the Tunbridge Wells to Hastings line was at Etchingham which is, from the railway point of view, near the start of the long climb north to Wadhurst. Here a staggered layout was provided, meaning that the 'up' and 'down' platforms were not opposite each other as was normal practice. The ornate canopy valance was unique to the S.E.R. and to a most attractive design. (Lens of Sutton)

Wadhurst station north of Etchingham with an early motor car on the station approach. The goods yard is full to capacity whilst an additional siding led back to some separate coal pens away from the yard on the extreme left hand side.   (Lens of Sutton)

In this view of the station the siding to the coal pens can be seen with the local merchant advertised as Messrs Cheeseman & Newington. A number of horse drays are to be seen backed up against the stabled wagons.

(Lens of Sutton)

Shunting wagons into the coal yard with an Ashford built 'C' class 0-6-0 engine.

(Lens of Sutton)

Busy times at the station, this time with a variety of horse cabs. From the number of people and especially children present this may have been the occasion of a special outing, possibly associated with the local Sunday School. (Lens of Sutton)

Inside the station proper we again find a layout with staggered platforms. The view is looking north towards Tunbridge Wells.

(Lens of Sutton)

A final view of Wadhurst station, this time from the south. In the distance another 'C' class 0-6-0 is shunting in the yard whilst the odd pieces of rail on the nearside bank may be evidence of recent relaying.

(Lens of Sutton)

Moving north to Frant and the last station prior to Tunbridge Wells. The first view, looking north, was taken in the late 19th century and shows a double sided signal as well as what appears to be an early signal cabin just off the end of the platform.

(Lens of Sutton)

A few years later and a canopy has been added to the 'down' side buildings along with a more substantial signal box. Under the canopy is a weighing machine, once a regular feature at most stations and used to assist in calculating the carriage charge on parcels traffic. This was another of the stopping places with staggered platforms and with access between the 'up' and 'down' lines for both passengers and staff by means of the board crossing. (Lens of Sutton)

The first railway to reach Tunbridge Wells came south from Tonbridge and was opened to a temporary station on 20th September 1845. Just over a year later the present station was opened and this is one of the earliest views of the site it has been possible to locate. In the right background is what appears to be a carriage with a vehicle being hand shunted towards it.

(Tunbridge Wells Museum)

A few years later and the buildings have been extended as well as a new platform provided. The early practice of supporting the canopy at regular intervals close to the platform edge can also be seen although there were disadvantages to this as carriage doors became wider and consequently sometimes hit a support if the door was opened when the train was moving.

(Reg Randell Collection)

The most recent view of the station taken in 1891 and viewed towards London. This time a footbridge and signal box have been added whilst at the end of the platform the wicker basket may well contain pigeons which were carried by the railway from very early on.

(Reg Randell Collection)

(12) Tunbridge Wells Station. SER. 30th Sept. 1891.

Hailsham Station. 473.

There were a number of north—south routes crossing the county, one of which was the line from Polegate heading north towards Tunbridge Wells — the construction of the line north of Eridge has already been detailed in the introductory photographs. First station north of Polegate was Hailsham, shown here looking south towards Eastbourne. On the left is the roof of a horsebox, whilst in the centre between the running lines is a board walk for railway staff.   (Lens of Sutton)

Hailsham station was on the route known as the Cuckoo line, a single track with passing loops at the stations. The view is seen towards London with a variety of contemporary enamel and other adverts under the canopy, including one of the most renowned for PEARS soap. The train is bound for Eastbourne. (Reg Randell Collection)

Situated in the midst of the Sussex countryside was Waldren & Horeham Road seen north towards Heathfield. On the back of the van is a board with the letters 'LV', it is thought this indicated 'Last Vehicle' and was used as an alternative to the more conventional tail lamp during the hours of daylight. The length of the train may mean this was a through Eastbourne to London working.

(Lens of Sutton)

Because of a difference in land levels the main buildings at Heathfield were on a different level to the track with access to the platforms via a series of steps. For the same reason the railway was also a little way from what was a market town which can be seen on the hill in the background.

(Lens of Sutton)

Heathfield Station, Ot

Rotherfield & Mark Cross was opened with the line to Polegate in 1880 and served a wide agricultural community. As would be expected then there were a number of sidings here, most of which appear well used.

(Reg Randell Collection)

Barcombe Mills station was on the line north east from Lewes towards Eridge and not to be confused with a similar sounding station on the nearby line to East Grinstead. This is looking north towards London and with the level crossing open for the railway.

(Lens of Sutton)

A similar view to the previous but one I could not resist including, principally because of the lovely sheeted wagon on the right. The vehicle is in fact covered with a tarpaulin which is supported by a centre rail. It was the practice for each local station to be served by a stopping goods train at least once daily which would then collect any wagons ready for movement toward their destination.

(Lens of Sutton)

Isfield station on the same route and now headquarters of the Primrose Line. Unusually the gates are only partly closed across the railway so it may have been this was a local practice at a time when road traffic was light.   (Lens of Sutton)

Isfield.   Sussex.

Isfield Station. L. B. & S. C. R.

A local service for Lewes leaving Isfield in charge of what may well be 'D' class tank No.290 'Denbies'. The main station building can be seen on the 'up' side whilst the other large structure further to the left is the former Station Inn later renamed the 'Laughing Fish'.   (Lens of Sutton)

One of the most important of the stations on the Eridge line was Uckfield, identified by having a footbridge for passengers to cross between the platforms when the level crossing was closed. The ornate canopy design of the L.B. & S.C.R. shows up again whilst the uppermost part of the building is in the favoured mock Tudor style. (Lens of Sutton)

Taken around the same period this view shows Uckfield at a somewhat busier time. In the background is the goods shed and office whilst there would appear to be a train at the platform partly hidden by the shadow of the overhanging tree.   (Lens of Sutton)

Inside the platforms at Uckfield with a comparison between light and shade. The first item of notice is the enamel sign affixed to the platform edge which states, *'Passengers are strictly forbidden to cross the line'* whilst a further notice above one of the doors reads 'George Alfred Parker — Station Clerk'. The scene is looking north towards Eridge and London. In the background is the level crossing which took the A22 London to Eastbourne road across the railway. In later years it was also the scene of long traffic jams.   (Lens of Sutton)

Associated for many years with a type of poultry this is Buxted station on the same line. Here the buildings are in a much simpler style and indeed apart from the canopy give little indication that it is a railway station. The premises on the left are a group of railway staff cottages with the station master living above the main station buildings.
(Lens of Sutton)

Probably taken around the turn of the century the camera has just caught the image of a train leaving the station for Uckfield and the south. The necessary time exposure required for early film emulsions has produced a blurred result.   (Lens of Sutton)

With a fair complement of passengers waiting, 'E4' tank No.466 'Honor Oak' arrives at Buxted with what is probably a Tunbridge Wells West to Brighton train via Lewes.
(Lens of Sutton)

Last station before Eridge was Crowborough, again with the distinctive station canopy. This is the bright and airy 'up' platform, in stark contrast to the railway stations of some other companies. The use of quantities of glass as part of the roof was a major feature of the station.   (Lens of Sutton)

Newick & Chailey Station. L. B. & S. C. R.

Without doubt the most famous line in East Sussex today must be the Bluebell Railway, which runs over part of the route formerly covered by the line from Culver Junction to East Grinstead. Unfortunately it was not possible for the preservationists to save all the line, Newick and Chailey being one of the stations that is but now a memory. In happier times a 'Terrier' tank is dwarfed by its single coach as it waits at the 'down' platform with a Lewes train.   (Lens of Sutton)

Like many railways the earthworks on the Bluebell railway were originally built for double track even though only a single line of rails was laid. The promoters had grand visions towards future expansion which somehow never came about. Instead there was a passing loop at most of the stopping places to enable trains to cross, whilst the station buildings were perhaps more in keeping with a main line than what was in effect a quiet backwater.   (Lens of Sutton)

Newick and Chailey Station. V85

Horsted Keynes, again on the Bluebell route, was also the junction for a short line running through Ardingly to Haywards Heath and as a result possessed a reasonable amount of siding space. During the early years of the century some was used for a rather sombre purpose with rows of engines awaiting either attention in Brighton works or the call to the scrapyard.   (Lens of Sutton)

North of East Grinstead a railway continued north towards Oxted and through the stations of Dormans and Lingfield both at one time within the county boundary of East Sussex. This particular line opened in 1884 with Dormans shown here probably around that time and awaiting its first trains.
(Lens of Sutton)

Of all the photographs gathered for this book I personally find this the most attractive. Something about the quiet charm of a rural station and with the evident peace and tranquillity so often missing from the busy lives we mostly lead today. The view is of the station entrance at Dormans with a small group posed for the camera. Notice also the letter box set into the station building. These were found at many rural stations which also doubled as Sub Post Offices. (Lens of Sutton)

Lingfield is of course associated with horse racing and consequently a number of extra facilities were provided to cater for the regular influx of race-goers. On the 'down' side the platform has been converted to an island with the far right hand face used for the special trains. Horse boxes were also dealt with whilst the provision of two footbridges is a further indication of the crowds handled.
(Lens of Sutton)

There were two stations between Lewes and Keymer Junction at Cooksbridge and Plumpton. This is Cooksbridge and seen towards London. In the background the wind-pump was used for drawing water from a deep well whilst the camera has also caught a young porter in the process of spinning a churn up the ramp of the platform.

(Reg Randell Collection)

Another station involved with 'the sport of Kings' was of course Plumpton, although here facilities were somewhat more modest. At the south end of the station was a level crossing controlled by a signal box visible in the next view. The level crossing gates were hand operated, their different styles an indication that one has probably been replaced, no doubt as a result of accident.

(Lens of Sutton)

Behind the signal box was a small milk factory, one of several similar facilities around the county prior to the advent of the major centralised dairy units. As well as the two dairymen a number of churns can be seen outside, the inked cross perhaps an indication of a previous accident.   (Lens of Sutton)

PLUMPTON. LBSCR

This time the scene is looking south and with part of the small yard on the left. It is interesting to compare the differing styles of the platform buildings at the various stations in the county as there would appear to be little in the way of a standard practice.

(Lens of Sutton)

A final view of Plumpton station, this time with a train passing over the level crossing bound for Haywards Heath. The roof of the signal box is rather ornate and includes a central belvedere in distinctive style. In 1987 this was one of the last remaining mechanical signal boxes in the area.   (Lens of Sutton)

Running east to west across the north of the county was the line from Tunbridge Wells to East Grinstead and Three Bridges. Much of the route was decidedly rural and exemplified by the station at Hartfield, the view towards Tunbridge Wells.   (Lens of Sutton)

Another delightfully named location was that of Forest Row and with considerably more in the way of facilities than at Hartfield. This is again looking east towards Tunbridge Wells, with a small goods yard in the distance beyond the signal box.   (Lens of Sutton)

Grange Road station served little more than a very localised community and consequently was only equipped with the most basic facilities. A good impression is gained of the heavy looking station canopy, far deeper than a number of other designs and this time without the meandering fascia. In the background two men are busy working on either the footbridge or the canopy whilst the station master stands on the platform, no doubt as supervisor.   (Lens of Sutton)

Just east of the platform was a small goods yard with access controlled from the signal box. On the extreme left is an end loading bank used when a private carriage was to be dealt with whilst the footbridge was later removed and re-erected at Sole Street.
(Lens of Sutton)